BEYOND THE SIDDHIS

Supernatural Powers and the Sutras of Patanjali

by

John McAfee

Credits

Editor: Ginny Ruths, Touchstone Publications

Production Manager: Pamela Jones

Production Assistants: Maria Deelman, Jen Irwin

Cover Design: Barbara A. Swanson

Design and Production: Graphics West, Inc., Colorado Springs, Colorado

Printer: Kendall Printing, Greeley, Colorado

Associate Publisher: Rogue Amazon Publications

2000 Arapaho Street
Woodland Park, Colorado 80863
EMAIL: support@woodlandpublications.com
WEBSITE: http://www.woodlandpublications.com

ISBN 0-9711569-3-X

CONTENTS

I do not know what I may appear to the world, but to myself I seem to have been only a boy playing by the seashore, and diverting myself in now and then finding a smoother pebble or a prettier shell than ordinary, while the great ocean of truth lay all undiscovered before me.

Sir Isaac Newton (1642–1727)

INTRODUCTION

A little more than 5,000 years ago, a race of people moved down from central Asia and settled in the Indus Valley of the Indian subcontinent. Little is known of their origin, but they brought with them a new science, previously unknown to the world. It was the science of the mind. These people possessed arts, technology, and a written language that contained the conceptual elements and images necessary for delving into the inner psyche. They were the Aryans, and their language was Sanskrit.

Interwoven within the Sanskrit language were both the conceptual elements of the human psyche—of consciousness—and the verbal constructs necessary to reveal this psyche. It was an astounding divergence from the language and science known at that time. Mankind had formerly occupied itself with the science of tools and the understanding of the external world—how to build, hunt, sow, reap, and attain physical security. The arrival of the Aryans shifted the emphasis to the *identity* of the builder, the hunter, the sower, the reaper.

They sought to understand the workings of individuals, as well as the things that they did. They were the first people to use a systematic science of enquiry to study their own natures.

From this enquiry into the nature of the self emerged a sophisticated system that we know today as the science of yoga. Its purpose was to create the foundation from which individuals may successfully answer the question, "Who am I?" The most striking aspect of yoga is how it has transcended time and culture. It has transported itself beyond the political, economic, social, and religious structures of a world vastly distant, both in concept and in time, from the modern world in which it now finds a comfortable home.

While the beginning roots of yoga are lost in the mists of time, we do have an enduring verbal description of the science dating back more than 2,500 years: "The Sutras of Patanjali." This writing is the foundation of all existing systems of yoga, and it is the most complete description of the science of self-enquiry that has survived from the Aryan pool of knowledge.

The word *sutra* literally means "thread," and Patanjali uses it to designate a line of thought. He wrote 195 sutras, divided into sections that address the nature of the body and its treatment, the nature of thoughts and their place in the process of living, the nature of consciousness, and the nature of the breath and its control. However, the third chapter of Patanjali's yoga sutras—generally referred to as the Siddhis—is the most esoteric and difficult to understand. This chapter on yogic powers, which includes instructions for learning seemingly impossible tasks such as levitation, invisibility, and the power to walk on water, has been used and misused through the centuries by occult practitioners, religious organizations, meditation groups, and anyone seeking magical or supernormal powers. Virtually all magic rituals, ceremonies, and practices in the modern world, through intermediate past masters, have their roots in the power sutras, and much of the New Age mysticism so popular today can be traced directly to Patanjali. The notions of divination, astral projection, clairvoyance, ESP, telepathy, conjuring, materialization, and channeling were first written about in the sutras, as were the concepts of the aura, spirit guides, inner planes, and nonphysical planes. Little of the modern world of mysticism does not trace its source back to the Siddhis section of the sutras.

The yogic powers described in the sutras obviously elicit scorn and disbelief from objective, scientific-minded persons; and just as obviously they entice those who seek something beyond the unsatisfying sphere of their own tiny realities. Yoga scholars, teachers, gurus, and practitioners have endlessly debated the meaning and intent of the Siddhis, and strong disagreement continues. What Patanjali truly intended is obscured by the cryptic style of his writing and by the inherent complexities of translating an ancient language whose words and structures are based on concepts that have no ready parallel in the modern world. But this much is certain: He was writing about a subject of ultimate importance, and he approaches it with grave seriousness. The fact that he dedicated 54 of the 195 sutras to the Siddhis suggests that it was not simply a fancy or a diversion. He had something specific in mind that had substantial importance for him, and therefore, we must assume, for the reader.

We can unlock this mystery, if we choose, through the simple process of self-observation, for the subject of the sutras is common to all of us. It is our selves. Whatever Patanjali was attempting to describe, the object of that description resides within us. Using his words as a pointer, we can look in the direction he indicates to see the reality that he could only coarsely represent with words. The intent of this book is to peel back the layer of words that hides the truth beneath the Siddhis.

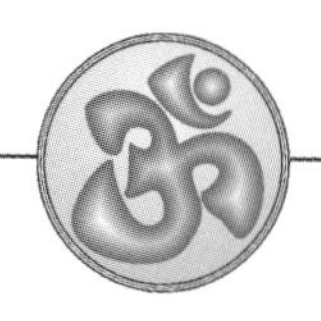

CHAPTER ONE

THE MYSTERY

What is life? It is the flash of a firefly in the night. It is the breath of a buffalo in the wintertime. It is the little shadow which runs across the grass and loses itself in the sunset.

Crowfoot, Blackfoot warrior and orator, 1890

One of the reasons that confusion and disagreement reign over the Siddhis is the fact that Patanjali contradicts himself throughout the discussion of the Siddhi powers. For example, he stresses the fact that all time is now—that the past is merely memory and the future does not exist. He affirms that the only reality is the reality in the moment, the now; yet in sutra 3.16 he instructs us in the process of divining the future. He implies throughout the sutras that the process of dividing and comparing the objects of perception is an impediment to self-knowledge, then in sutra 3.52 he tells us how to develop the power to divide things that are indivisible. He states that consciousness has no locality, yet in 3.39 he describes how to transfer that consciousness into the localized body of another. The Siddhis exude contradictions. But perhaps the greatest contradiction is in the spirit of the powers themselves.

Patanjali states in the beginning sutras that the purpose of yoga is liberation. The point is to reach self-understanding, thus breaking the bonds of conditioning. Patanjali describes self-understanding as a state of oneness with life, a union with God, a state of perfection.

His aim with the sutras is to provide readers with the tools and understanding necessary to reach this state. Yet in sutra 3.38, he says plainly that the Siddhis—those powers he actively directs us to pursue—are obstacles to this liberation: impediments on the path to enlightenment and union with life. Finally, in the last few sutras of the Siddhis, after he has instructed us in detail on the techniques required to gain all of these powers, he states, "By abandoning the quest for these powers, liberation becomes possible." It seems to be the height of contradiction.

Why would Patanjali dedicate nearly a third of the sutras to a set of instructions that, if followed, virtually guarantee failure as measured by his own aim? If the quest for and attainment of these powers is a detriment, why mention them at all, except possibly for a brief comment to the effect that if you currently levitate or make yourself invisible, then please stop doing so.

Commentators and various gurus throughout the centuries have attempted to resolve the contradiction by saying that the powers in and of themselves are not a detriment, but that our attachments to them, once we attain them, create the problem. Thus, they argue, if we can attain the powers and remain unattached to them, then all will be well. This interpretation sounds very neat and logical, except for the following problem: Why do we want these powers to begin with? We can certainly reach

self-understanding without learning how to walk on water or to become as small as an atom. Our own greeds, desires, ambitions, deceptions, and jealousies surely cannot become more visible as we become physically smaller or more adept at floating. Our true natures are plainly present, grossly visible, and they are our constant companions. Our inability to levitate does not keep us from seeing them; it is our fear that blinds us. If we look at any desire for power, we see that the attachment is in the original desire. The ego wants such powers in order to expand itself. Thus the quest for the powers begins with attachment, and because in all actions the end contains the means, we will end up with this same attachment. To believe that the ego will contradict its own nature after it has reached omnipotence (sutra 3.49) is absurd.

Patanjali is using a subtle but simple sleight of hand in all of this. We can see it clearly if we are willing to drop all of our prejudices, one way or another, about the validity or the meaning of the Siddhis.

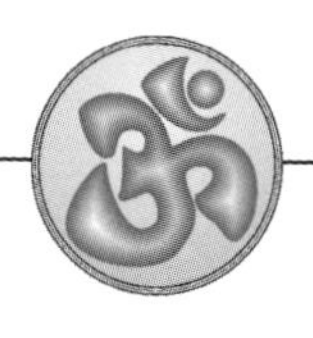

CHAPTER TWO

ATTAINMENTS

Perfection is achieved, not when there is nothing more to add, but when there is nothing left to take away.

Antoine de Saint-Exupéry
(1900–1944)

"The Siddhis" was not the title that Patanjali gave to his third section on the powers. He called it the "Vibhuti Pada." Time and custom have converted it to "The Siddhis" in most commentaries, since the word *siddhi*, meaning "perfection," seemed to the Western mind more indicative of the powers outlined in the section. But there is a profound difference in meaning between the two titles. *Vibhuti Pada* literally means "the section on attainments." Consequently, Patanjali seems to indicate that the following sutras related to attainments or perhaps the process of attaining. One might of course attain perfection, but attainments do not necessarily equate to perfection. The difference may appear subtle or insignificant, but it is nevertheless profound, as we shall see.

The root of the word *vibhuti* is "to become." The significance is this: All attainments are becomings. When we attain power, we become powerful. When we attain wealth, we become wealthy. When we attain spirituality, we become spiritual. Attainment *is* becoming. Whatever we attain, we attach it to ourselves and it becomes an extension of our self-image —an identification of the ego. Whether we attain strength, knowledge, or celibacy, it becomes a part of the ego. The ego celebrates the fact that it has become strong, knowledgeable, or celibate.

Therefore, unless Patanjali was deliberately misleading us, he intended his third chapter to address the issue of attainments and the process of attaining—the self's process of becoming. The Siddhis have the deepest focus of all of the sutras, because the process of becoming is intricately woven into the nature of time and the mechanics of thought, both of which ultimately support the fabric of fear —which is the barrier to self-awareness. We will delve into this concept in detail as we proceed, but first we need to address the driving force in the process of becoming: our insufficiencies.

We are insufficient to the task of living. Please look deeply and truthfully at yourself, and you will see this obvious truth. We are empty, fearful, lonely, and isolated. We have

separated ourselves from the world and constructed barriers to isolate ourselves even further. We imitate those whom we believe know more than ourselves, and shun those whom we judge to be of no value to our own ambitions or pleasures. We are fearful of death, and of living. We tie together pleasure, security, and need and we call this package love. We are self-centered and concerned with our own welfare, even to the detriment of nearly everyone else. We have constructed a world based on possessiveness and ambition. If we are honest, we see that we are empty shells, acting out a poor imitation of living.

From this reality of loneliness we reach out and try, through attainments, to fill our emptiness with possessions, power, wealth, the love of others, knowledge, talents, and prestige. It is a vain process, for this emptiness is the absence of love—not the love of romance novels, but the love that blooms when we see the reality of ourselves, with our full being, and we free ourselves from our self-imposed bondage. That love is truth, beauty, reality, oneness. No possession, no power, no amount of money, no social status or prestige can fill the void created by the absence of this love. This emptiness is the driving force of attainment, and it is the root of our never-ending desire to become what we are not.

It is clear, if we look closely and without fear, that this process of endless becoming, of endlessly attaining, is an obstacle in the process of self-understanding. We can only know ourselves in relationship to the present moment. It is how we act, feel, and think in the reality of the now that shows us who we are. Our gestures, words, and expressions in our moment-to-moment relationship with life are the mirror in which we can see ourselves. If we are endlessly becoming something —more spiritual, more knowledgeable, wiser, wealthier—then we are never fully present. The present thus becomes a tool that we use

to create some future reality in which we will be something different. We are unable to live the present because we use it rather than live it; the present is filled with thoughts of the future. But we are what we are. We can never be what we are not until we see fully, with heart and mind, with our full being, the reality of ourselves. That awareness is itself the force of change.

If you look into yourself, with uncompromising honesty, to find the meaning of Patanjali's attainments, that meaning will become clear. We will address some of the individual sutras in the following section. The sheer volume precludes a comprehensive discussion of them all, but their root is the same in every case. We will address enough of them that you can apply the principles to the rest on your own if you are so inclined.

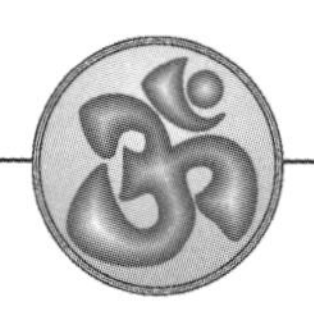

CHAPTER THREE

MASTERY OF TIME

But at my back I
always hear
Time's winged chariot
hurrying near;
And yonder all before
us lie
Deserts of vast eternity.

Andrew Marvell, (1621–1678)

Sutra 3.16 states that, through proper practice, we can learn to see either the past or the future as if it were actually happening in the present.

If we were to remove this sutra from the context of Patanjali's powers and simply look at it objectively, what would we see? Is there anything in this sutra that we can relate to our own existence? Does it shed light on any internal process, any part of our being? Please, look within yourself; it is a serious issue and requires a serious enquiry.

Clearly, this sutra describes an activity that we already practice. We constantly see the past and the future, fantasizing future realities and rehashing the past in an unending cycle within our minds. While driving to work we relive the morning's experiences or visualize what we will do when we get to the office. We imagine our vacations before we live them, and recreate them in our minds long after we have returned to our everyday grind. We anticipate what we will eat at the restaurant before we sit down at the table. We envision the outcome of a romantic date before we even meet the person. We replay an unsatisfactory experience, changing it in various ways to create the reality of what we should or could have done. This is our life. In fact, we are seldom in the present. The present is merely an opportunity to plan, anticipate, fantasize, rework, or restructure our past or future realities. We are constantly bringing the past or the future into the present. We are masters of time travel.

Do you see the sublime, awesome humor of the man who wrote this sutra? He implies that with proper training, we can learn to do that which we are unable not to do. See the beauty of this! Try, for only one minute, to stop living in the past or the future. It will not be possible. Your thoughts will invariably drift to one fantasy or another—either a future circumstance or a past experience. Just try it for one minute; it is a simple and quick experiment.

Patanjali certainly recognized that our constant forays into the past and the future are impediments to self-knowledge. The self exists in the present. Our actions, thoughts, and feelings are in the present. The world that we must relate to exists now, in the present. Until we stop living outside of the present moment, we can never be in the here and now. And if we are not fully aware in the now, then we will never be able to see the self that exists in this infinite reality of the moment.

We are caught in this state because we have divided life into past, present, and future, and we treat these divisions as if they had an inherent reality. But this assumption is false. Only the eternal now exists. We have divided time because we are empty and we think that the emptiness can be filled through the process of becoming—becoming happier, wiser, more spiritual, more powerful. And we can only become something else if we have a past and a future. We use our past experience and mold it in the present to achieve a future result. That is our never-ending occupation. But true change can only happen in the moment. If we cannot change now, completely, instantly, then we will never change. The process of becoming is an illusion, a deception. We deceive ourselves into believing that through time we will gradually change hatred into compassion, greed into nonattachment, and fear into joy. But such change is merely postponed by the act of becoming. We say we will change tomorrow through the process of discipline, by increasing our knowledge or through the power of will. But discipline and will merely strengthen the quality that they attempt to eradicate. We use anger to remove anger: we are angry that we have anger and we must be rid of it. We use desire to rid ourselves of desire: we desire the state of desirelessness. Our mental constructs are such an absurdity. We can only remove anger and desire by

seeing the reality of our current condition. We must see, with our full being, the source, the action, and the results of desire as it is occurring in the moment. Such awareness is the action that dissolves desire and frees us from both desire and its opposite. And this action is instantaneous.

The true beauty of Patanjali's writing is that when we stop living in the past and future, when we stop creating images in our minds and living within them, then all time becomes now. The past and the future are folded into the present and then we see clearly—not through images and fantasies, but through the actuality of living—the past, the future, and the present as one moving reality, exactly as described in the sutra. Such is the case with all of the Siddhis. They describe our current reality, and when we see that reality fearlessly, with dcpth and clarity, our poor reality evaporates. In its place is the real, the true, in which we can live fully.

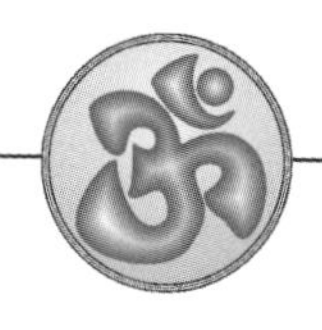

CHAPTER FOUR

KNOWLEDGE OF THE MIND

If you gaze long into the abyss, the abyss will gaze back into you.

Friedrich Nietzsche
(1844–1900)

Sutra 3.21 tells us how, with appropriate practice, we may know the nature of any person's mind from the image of that person's form.

This sutra is used, obviously, in attempts to develop the power to read minds, for whatever purpose. Crystal gazers, magicians of every type, charlatans, and ordinary people have delved into this sutra with the hope that they will attain the power to see the hidden thoughts of their fellow man. For myself, I am happy to be oblivious of my neighbor's fancies, but for many, the lure of such power is irresistible.

What is the truth of this sutra? Can we look into our own hearts and minds and see the simple reality that Patanjali describes? It is a universal truth for all who are living in the bondage created by the ego. Please, look into yourself. It is not enough to be given the answer without truly questioning; the truth that you perceive with the fullness of yourself,

after deep enquiry, is the only one that can be true for you. If you are given an answer and grasp it intellectually, you only have intellectual knowledge, and it will be of little use to you.

How do we relate to people—to our spouse, boss, neighbors, relatives, the clerk at the grocery store? We create images of them, and based on the nature of that image we form a relationship. We take all of our past hurts, pleasures, or angers that resulted from our relationship with the person and we add them to our image. That image becomes our reality, and it is the image to which we relate. Please, see this in yourself. It is enormously important to see that this is how we relate to the world.

We further distort the reality of those around us by projecting ourselves onto the image that we create of them. If we have an image of ourselves as being eloquent and charming, for example, then we interpret politeness in others as interest in ourselves. Someone may listen to our dialogue with an intent look and a smile while hoping we will soon shut up, yet we perceive the attention as evidence of our irresistible charisma. We form an image of that person as someone who is truly interested in us, and we feel warmth toward that image. If we have an image of ourselves as sexually desirable, even irresistible, then we will interpret even a glance from someone who interests us as a look of desire. We ascribe hidden meanings to their words and form an image of them as possible sexual partners. If we are proud, then we imagine that others admire us and hear flattery as sincerity.

If we believe ourselves to be a great guru or teacher, we see devotion and awe in those around us. If we are paranoid, we find hostility and threat in people's actions and form images of them as menacing and aggressive.

Thus we interpret the actions and words of those around us according to our own self-image. We do this because others' actions and words have significance to us only to the extent that they affect us. We are self-centered; our concern is only for ourselves. We are interested in how people treat us, think of us; whether they stay with us or leave us; whether they love us or hate us; whether they comfort us, support us, entertain us; whether they keep us from being lonely or isolated. The image that we create of others is in reality a projection of ourselves. We do not truly relate to another; we relate only to a projection of our self with which we clothe the other person.

If you can see this process in yourself, then you will realize that we are constantly reading others' minds. We anticipate how our spouse will react to a request, and may even become angry before our request is denied. We see a certain look in a person's face and we interpret

it to our liking—we "know" what they are thinking. Because we see images, not people, and because we ourselves have created these images, we are omniscient. The images are our creations and we have full power over their composition and intents. But how can we ever truly know another while we create images as barriers to knowing?

This is the question Patanjali puts to us. We must stop this insane process of creating images. If we live in a world of images, then we live entirely within our own minds—the world eludes us and life is perpetual emptiness. It is when we stop believing that we know another, when we allow the mystery of every person to unfold without anticipation, that the fullness of life begins. We must abandon past hurts and pleasures and at every moment meet each person anew. If we are thus able to open ourselves up to life, then we transcend the need to read another's mind, because we see that we *are* the other. We see that all people have identical feelings: the same hurts, fears, longings, and hopes, the same structure of thinking and self-centered concerns. We grasp the nature of all minds because we are all one mind, not as some vague concept, but as a concrete reality. Such is the true nature of reality that blossoms into being when we stop reading minds.

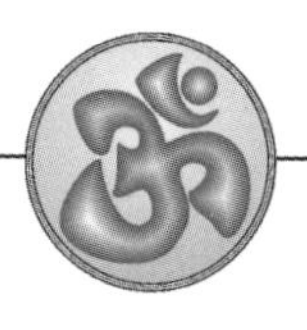

CHAPTER FIVE

KNOWLEDGE OF DEATH

Behold, now I am become Death, the destroyer of worlds.

Lord Krishna in the Bhagavad Gita

Sutra 3.23 shows us how we can attain the foreknowledge of our own death.

It is no surprise that this is not the most popular of the Siddhi powers. Foreknowledge of death is not something that people generally clamor for. Quite the contrary, most of us live as though death were a distant dream, with no real impact on our existence. It might seem odd that Patanjali includes this attainment as one of the powers; it is the only one that has no direct application to living. Levitating or walking on water could possibly be put to some use, but where is the utility in knowing about our own death?

As with the other attainments, more than one meaning hides behind this sutra. Patanjali tells us that we can develop the power to know our own death, but at some level inside ourselves, we already have that power. We use this power to expand our illusion of security and self-continuity. Observe your actions in your day-to-day living. Do we not act as if we know, with certainty, that death is a distant event? Certainly we do. Could you honestly claim to act the same if you believed—truly believed—that you *might* die in the next week, the next day, or the next hour? Of course not. Your life would be radically different. Anger and resentment would disappear; you would see them as the ludicrous vanities that they are. All your superfluous ambitions, drives, and jealousies would evaporate. Your possessiveness of material things would immediately fall away. Your drive for security would cease. Yet, such an onslaught of truth does not happen in our lives. Each of us lives and behaves as though we know, factually and unequivocally, that we will be around tomorrow.

Intellectually, of course, we know that death may occur at any moment. We can rationalize it and even speak glibly about the possibility that our lives may suddenly cease. We buy life insurance to protect our families in the event of our death, and we write our wills. But we quickly forget these necessities and allow the reality of death to fade into the background. The knowing of the intellect is subservient to the ego and has but slight long-term importance. Such intellectual knowledge has little power to change the image that we have of ourselves. In spite of the intellect, the ego has created an image of itself as continuous

through time. This image is what matters. The ego fears death and structures its image so that death plays no real part in its relationship to the world. To do so, it must place death at a distance, creating an unspoken "knowing" in relation to death. This knowing may be unconscious, but it exists, and it is evident in all our relationships with the world.

If you look into yourself, you will see this conviction of the remoteness of your own death. Your every thought, act, and feeling, your very being reveals the existence of this conviction, which manifests as some ill-defined belief, faith, or image of yourself continuing to exist. Do you see the image of yourself as concretely existing in subsequent moments of time? This image tells you not to concern yourself with death: that death is, and will remain, a distant event.

This hidden conviction gives the ego freedom to continue indefinitely the process of becoming, the process of attainment. With death at a distance, we have time for change, time for the actions of will, discipline, and desire to have their effects. Thus this conviction is the source of illusion and the cause of suffering, for we cannot be present to the reality of

ourselves while we are simultaneously becoming something else. But there is no time as past and future, so each moment of living is also a dying. We cannot relegate death to a position of remoteness. It is woven into the fabric of life. We keep the past alive through the illusion of memory, but the past is, in truth, dead. Each moment of reality, through its infinite movement, leaves the dead past in its wake.

When we learn to die to the past, when we bring the process of dying into the process of living, then death takes on a new meaning. It cannot be separated from beauty, from life, and the tension between living and dying is replaced with the flowering of immortality.

Patanjali says that we can achieve knowledge of our own death. When we end the illusion that death is a distant event, we know death in each moment of life. We watch the exquisite beauty of a sunset and then it is gone. We do not hold on to it, or desire more, or hope for a repeat of the event. It is simply gone; we die to it, as we die to each and every moment of life, as truth and beauty move with infinite grace in an everlasting unfolding. When death thus becomes a companion to living, we have no fear of it. There is no past, and therefore no attachment, possession, or sense of continuity that we can lose. Time ceases, and thus the finality of death is ended.

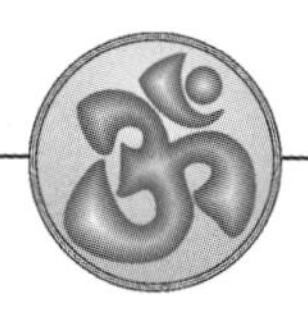

CHAPTER SIX

SUPER-SENSORY PERCEPTION

Though our brother is on the rack, our senses will never inform us of what he suffers.

Adam Smith (1723–1790)

Sutra 3.37 describes how we can attain the powers of more than natural hearing, touch, sight, taste, and smell. "More than natural" is a literal translation. Most translators use the word *supernatural* to describe these powers of the senses, but this term can have connotations far beyond the root meaning of the ancient Sanskrit text. Translations more in spirit with the text might be "beyond natural senses" or "beyond normal senses"; some translators have even chosen "exaggerated senses" to impart the meaning.

We don't need to debate the specifics of word choice, because the focus and intent of this sutra become perfectly clear if we simply look at the reality of our relationship to our own senses. Such clarification is Patanjali's intent for each of the sutras—to motivate us to enquire within so as to see the truth. Undeniably, all of us have exaggerated the importance of our senses. We live lives of increasing sensuality and decreasing joy. We satiate one of our senses and quickly move to another in an incessant rotation. We overeat, or we inflate the importance of sex, or we visually and aurally stimulate ourselves through nonstop music, television, movies, or video games. We stimulate ourselves through drugs and alcohol, and through excitements of various kinds. When such entertainments are unavailable, we move into the realm of thought and continue the stimulation through fantasy and imaginings, reliving our past stimulations or creating future scenarios for ourselves. Sensation is the driving force of our desires and the source of our pleasures. We have exaggerated them, made them greater than normal, greater than natural. In this spirit we could indeed call them supernatural.

Our senses are our tools of perception. Through hearing, taste, touch, sight, and smell we know the world; they allow us to relate to life. Our knowledge of and relationship to nature, the material world, and other people depend on the appropriate use of these senses. When we stretch our senses beyond the realm of perception and into the realm of pleasure, perception itself suffers; while we are stimulating our senses for self-gratification, we cannot simultaneously use them to perceive truth and reality. If we dull our brain with drugs, for example, we may feel a momentary pleasure, but the brain cannot at the same time be a clear and effective instrument of perception. What we perceive will be clouded and less than the truth. Thus, we alienate ourselves from reality.

Throughout the sutras, Patanjali refers to *awareness* as both the means of freedom and the result of freedom. It is the key to truth, beauty, and the infinite reality that he describes as the true nature of life. True awareness of the moment—of the flight of a bird, the distant stars, an ocean wave, the cry of a baby, or the human song—is the source of joy, ecstasy, and bliss. It is based on the senses, yet it has nothing to do with pleasure, which is sought after, self-generated, imitative, and intertwined with thought. By using the senses as instruments of perception, without the interference of thought or the ego, we can perceive and understand reality: We can become aware, and from that pure awareness springs the joy of truth and beauty. However, when we make the senses a slave to our desires, we turn our backs on reality and begin living in illusion—the self-created illusion of senses perverted. We then sense only the limited imaginings of our minds instead of the infinite movement of reality.

If we can see, with our full hearts and minds, the truth of our inflated use of our senses, then the illusion that we have created shatters. We cease, instantly, the misuse, and a different perception begins. In this new perception, our senses do indeed become supernatural: not in a distorted, alienating manner, but in a way that unifies experience. Perception is no longer narrow and exclusive. We are able to see, hear, and touch reality in its fullness.

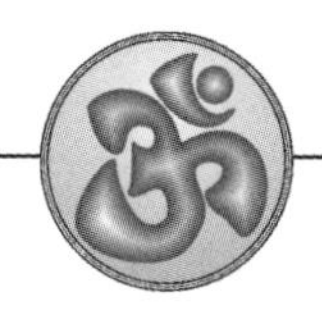

CHAPTER SEVEN

PROJECTION OF CONSCIOUSNESS

Few are those who see with their own eyes and feel with their own hearts.

Albert Einstein (1879–1955)

Sutra 3.38 explains how we can attain the power to transfer our consciousness into the body of another.

This sutra is one of the most subtle, requiring great sensitivity of mind in order to perceive its intent. Before we can delve into it, we must understand the nature and substance of consciousness.

What is this individual consciousness that we might wish to transfer to the body of another? Patanjali clearly implies "the consciousness of the yogi," so the consciousness he refers to must be individual, localized, possessed of ourselves. It must have some relationship to our individual sense of "I." And what is that relationship? Is consciousness a possession of the "I;" or is the "I" a possession of consciousness; or is consciousness, in fact, separate and distinct from that sense of "I?"

If you observe your thoughts and perceptions you will see that consciousness always has an object. You are conscious *of* things. Each of us is conscious of our environment, of feelings, of thoughts, of light and dark, of sounds, touch, and smells. Consciousness appears to be separate from the objects of which it is conscious—a distinct entity or capacity of the self. But is it separate from the "I" that perceives, thinks, chooses, wills, and desires? With quiet, sensitive self-observation, you will find that consciousness *is* the sense of "I;" they cannot be separated. But this consciousness is not the *awareness* that Patanjali addresses. Awareness has no object and no separate entity that is aware. Awareness comes into being when the sense of "I" as a separate entity ceases. With the cessation of individual consciousness, an awareness that has no center, no point that is aware of any other point, becomes possible. Such awareness is of the totality, not of the individual.

Individual consciousness is separative and divisive. The thought, "I am conscious of something" separates that consciousness from the world, dividing the world into the "I" and the objects of which the "I" is conscious. Based on the divisive process of thinking, consciousness is always accompanied by thought.

In fact, consciousness cannot be separated from thought; they are one. The "I," consciousness, and thought are a unitary entity. Thought has divided itself into the thinker and the thought, the chooser and the choice, the actor and the act. This thinker, actor, and chooser is consciousness, the "I." But this consciousness cannot be separated from thought because it has been created by thought.

It is this consciousness, this segment of thought, which Patanjali tells us we can learn to project into the body of another. Yet, it is obvious that we are already engaged in this process. Not only do we project our consciousness into all the people that we meet; all of them are at the same time projecting their consciousness into us.

Our consciousness is made up of the past: our experiences, memories, knowledge, hurts, and pleasures. Our ideals, our worldview, our affiliations, our preferences, and our personal idiosyncrasies are molded and conditioned by the culture in which we were raised. This culture—composed of parents, schools, newspapers, television, movies, books, friends, bosses, families, political structures, and so on—provides, intact, a structure of thinking and the substance of consciousness. When we attempt to sway others to our way of thinking, we impress our consciousness onto them. We want them to think as we think, feel as we feel, see things as we see them; depending upon our charisma and ability to influence, we modify their "seeing" of the world. A piece of our consciousness imparts itself to them.

Further, our consciousness is influenced by everyone and everything we come in contact with. It is colored by the ideas and concepts imparted by others: by the media, by politics, and by social and economic events. We see good where there was bad, or value where none existed before. The rise of a new political ideology may change our perceptions of poverty, greed, or business; we may alter our concept of a proper diet based on new nutritional advice; our appreciation of beauty is enhanced by education in the arts. Consciousness is ever at the whim of thought. Ideas mold our seeing of the world. We become whatever influences us the most. We are imitators of ideas.

This is the illusion Patanjali wants us to see. Our consciousness is ever changing, ever influenced by the ideals of the world; it must be, because consciousness is created and maintained in the realm of thought. But reality is simply what it is. It is not open to interpretation or to comparison between competing ideals. Truth is simply truth; it is the actuality of life, without judgments, choice, or points of view. Our creation of ideals gives us points of view, but the ideal is not the actual. The ideal is how we think the world *should* or *could* be, how people *should* or *could* act. When we seek the ideal, we abandon the truth—the reality of the present moment.

However, when we stop allowing the world to impart its consciousness into ourselves, when we abandon our arrogance and our attempts to influence others to our way of thinking, then a new awareness dawns. Our individual consciousness comes to an end, and something indefinable begins. Some have called this new awareness a universal consciousness, or a cosmic consciousness, but these words are dangerous. From our experience of individual consciousness, we think of consciousness as having a perceiver, some entity that is conscious of something; but in this new awareness without individual consciousness, there is no perceiver, and no object of perception. There is simply awareness.

Words are a danger. When we speak of consciousness or awareness, the words are only representations of something that cannot be known through words. They point to a reality that lies far beyond words. It is important that we not get caught up in words, ideas, and images, but rather move beyond them to the reality that they represent. It is the idea or concept of truth that we create in our minds—our belief that we know reality before we perceive it—which keeps us in darkness.

Patanjali's words direct us to this reality: There is no consciousness without thought, and true awareness lies beyond thought. Experiment with this potential and you will experience the profound change that occurs when

we are merely acting, perceiving, without the central point of the "I"—without thought. Consciousness creates distance between itself and its object; it must do so to exist as a separate entity. And this distance is what separates us from the infinite movement of life, from the present moment. When we abandon thought and consciousness, we will see the deep truth of this sutra. We are all, in truth, one consciousness. Nothing separates your consciousness from that of any other. To this degree our consciousness is, and has always been, inside the body of all people.

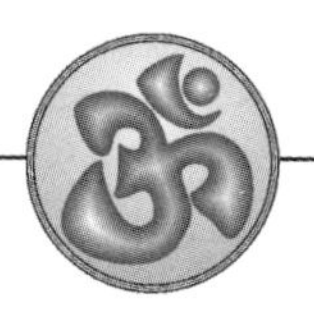

CHAPTER EIGHT

INVISIBILITY

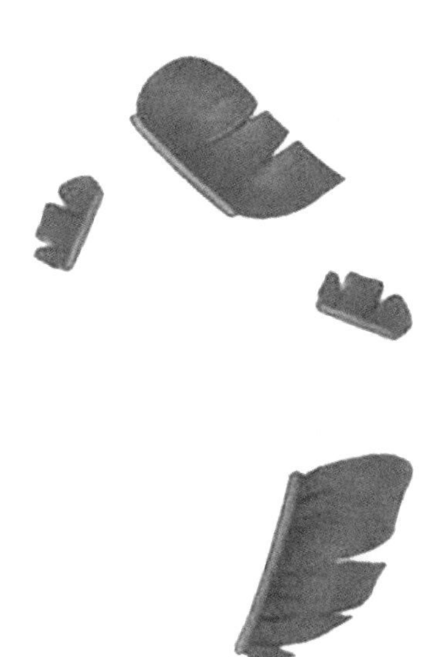

It is only with the heart that one can see rightly. What is essential is invisible to the eye.

Antoine de Saint-Exupéry
(1900–1944)

Sutra 3.21 is a favorite of many seekers. It says that we can attain the power to become invisible. How many would not like that ability? To be able to disappear, to avoid the piercing gaze of the world, to indulge our whims without being seen or caught, is certainly an attractive thought.

However, before we spend years practicing the formula for attainment that Patanjali provides, we might first ask ourselves how visible we are now. Though you may think the question is ludicrous and not worthy of consideration, it is in fact not absurd. If you will consider it seriously and without preconceptions, you will find a startling answer. As for me, I say that few of us are visible to any degree whatsoever, but what I say cannot help anyone. You must experiment with the question yourself and come to an answer on your own for it to have any true meaning. Otherwise, you will merely have my definitions, which are of little value to you.

Ask yourself, first, whether you can see any part of yourself. We can leave for later the question of what others see of you; it is less important and much easier to answer after you discern your ability to see yourself.

When you look at yourself, what do you see? Do you see the reality of yourself, which for most is a self-centered, narrow existence, full of fear and conflict? Most of us are unable to see the reality of our lives, and instead see what we want to see. We interpret our actions, feelings, and thoughts so that they support not reality, but the image that we carefully construct of ourselves. This image is crafted by the ego to veil the underlying emptiness of our being. If we saw ourselves as we are, most of us would see an empty, confused existence driven by fear, desire, and unsatisfied aspirations. We would see a field of suffering and anguish punctuated by brief moments of pleasure.

Let's look at something simple, like ambition. Most of us perceive the fact that we are ambitious. We work to get ahead; to get a better job, more knowledge, or social prestige; or to be able to afford a better home, car, or some other material object. We can see our ambition and acknowledge the fact that we act on it. But how many of us see that our ambition is merely the outer manifestation of our inner fear and emptiness? We fear poverty and thus strive for security. We envy those with more than ourselves and struggle to surpass them. Whatever our ambition, if we trace it to its roots we will find an emptiness that we attempt to fill with success, power, or security. The emptiness is our reality, and the ideal offered by our ambition is the thing that we are not. We see the ideal, but the reality is hidden to us.

Let's consider our sense of compassion —our caring for others. We may see ourselves as compassionate or caring. We may occupy ourselves with charities or with volunteer work for those less fortunate. We may join organizations that promote social improvement or donate time or money to causes that help the poor or politically oppressed. However, ask yourself this simple question: Would you feel just as satisfied in your endeavors if you gave your time or money totally anonymously? Not just anonymous to the public, but also to your family, friends, associates, neighbors, and social acquaintances. Imagine yourself giving to the less fortunate exactly as you do now, but not a soul in the world knows it—not even the recipients of your giving. If you are honest with yourself, you will feel minimal satisfaction with this concept. It's true that some of us

give anonymously, but most do not also keep the secret from their spouse, close friends, and associates. If we observe ourselves carefully, without fear or judgment, we will find that deep inside we are satisfying one or another of our selfish needs through our charity. We want to belong, so we achieve a sense of belonging through our participation in charitable organizations. Or we seek prestige, so we want others to know that we act on our social conscience. Or we feel a genuine discomfort when we see the poor and downtrodden, and seek to alleviate that discomfort through our charitable actions. But if we truly had compassion for others, would we stop at these tiny gestures? No, we would dedicate our entire lives to others. That is what compassion implies—the recognition of our own complete unimportance in the face of large-scale world suffering.

Our lives are empty, yet we create the illusion of fullness through our nonstop activities, entertainments, pleasures, and daydreams—and we believe the illusion. We are petty, yet we perceive ourselves as magnanimous and gracious. We are filled with greed, yet we believe that we are generous and helpful. We are jealous and envious of others, yet we see ourselves as accepting and loving. Fear and anxiety consume us, yet we clothe ourselves in false bravery and indifference. And we believe the false image that we have created.

Thus our lives are pure illusion. We have created a self-image with the purpose of hiding our fundamental realities, and this image is all that we see. We do not see the truth of our being. The reality of ourselves is invisible to us. If we are honest with ourselves, we will recognize this invisibility. But how do others see us?

As we create self-images that hide our true identities, so we also create images of others that bolster our own image. We are insecure in our self-image; we must be, because reality cannot support our self-image. It is molded by ideals, by how things might be, by how we should behave and feel, and this molding is in constant conflict with our true natures. To support this unreal structure, our self-image projects itself onto others and creates correspondingly unreal images of them. These images are created by our self-image in its own image. If we are insecure and someone flatters us, we interpret the flattery as genuine interest in us. We begin to construct an image of the other based on this unreality, adding to it only those elements that support our own image. This image of the person is what we see, not the underlying reality. Thus for most of those around us, their own process of image-making ensures that we remain invisible to them.

Patanjali urges us to see the reality of our image-making. His point is that as long as we make images, our true natures will remain invisible. When we cease this process then we see, not just ourselves, but everyone, as we are in actuality. A new awareness emerges, in which we see that separateness and division do not exist. What we see as the form of another is in reality ourselves. The individuality of ourselves, and of others, then becomes invisible in its truest meaning.

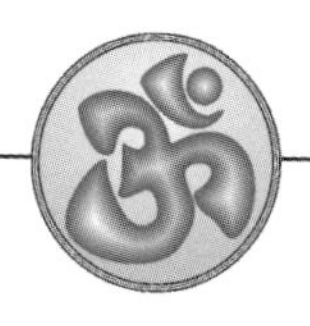

CHAPTER NINE

OMNIPOTENCE

I *condemn no man — only man's belief in his own omnipotence.*

Paramahansa Yogananda

Sutra 3.50 has generally been referred to as the *omnipotence* sutra, but "supremacy" is closer to a literal translation. It describes how we may attain the power of supremacy over all beings. Patanjali places this modest sutra immediately before the one that warns us against attaining any of the powers, so it might seem to have special significance. Indeed, if we look into this sutra carefully, we will see that all of the sutras can be folded into this one.

To open the door to this sutra, we only need to ask ourselves the following question: What is the one thing that most concerns us in life—the thing above all else that we find most interesting, that is always our number one occupation? It is ourselves. Look within with openness and honesty, and you will find that we are, each one of us, interested primarily in ourselves.

Our lives revolve around *our* pleasures, *our* fears, *our* hurts, *our* desires, *our* families, *our* jobs, and *our* homes. Our decisions in life are predicated on how the outcomes affect us, and our actions, thoughts, and feelings relate to our own ambitions and ideals. Our own families are more important to us than the families of others, and our families' losses and hurts affect us more than the losses of others. Further, whatever we desire for others is ultimately for our own satisfaction. If we desire something for a loved one, we really desire it for our own fulfillment—we identify with our loved ones and take personal satisfaction in their attainments. We beam with joy when our children are happy and feel pride and delight if our spouse gets a better job—it is *our* joy, *our* pride and delight. It is enormously important that we see this truth of ourselves. You may say such behavior is normal, and that would certainly be true; nevertheless, it clearly indicates that we are more concerned with the sphere of our own lives than with the rest of mankind. The fact that everyone else behaves in the same way does not negate our own self-centeredness.

If we believe that something is true, then in our hearts we "know" it is true, and anything that contradicts our truth is obviously false. Thus, we have *our* moralities and ideals, and whatever *we* feel is right, we try to impose on the world. We know how people should behave and are quick to determine what is right and what is wrong with the world. We judge people's actions, their speech, their dress and grooming, their knowledge and

opinions, and we are certain that the world would be better if they acted, talked, dressed, and believed as we do.

We form conclusions about life from our own experience, and those conclusions become reality for us. It doesn't matter that our tiny experience can only be a meaningless fraction of life; our lives are nevertheless supremely important when compared to the experience and conclusions of others. Our conclusions are the truth, and the differing conclusions of others are in error.

If we observe ourselves in our relationship to the world, most of us will quickly see our supremacy over everyone else. We do not need to practice this sutra in order to attain such supremacy—it is, at this very moment, the core of our being. But we must, at all costs, end it. This sense of our own supremacy is the root of violence and suffering in the world. It is the source of individual arrogance and hatred, and the cause of our indifference to the anguish of others. Theft and muggings occur because thieves have supremacy over their victims; their needs outweigh the needs of the rest of the world. All crimes—all relationships —have the same basis. Our ambitions allow us to achieve success at the cost of our competitors. We may feel sorry for the losers, but we are tremendously happy at our success, and our own happiness outranks the happiness of our competition. In this aspect, we are no different from thieves.

Furthermore, in the larger world this supremacy inflates to appalling proportions. Nations, states, political parties, and religious and social organizations are creations of the individual. As is the individual, so are the collective creations of the individual. Collective supremacy is the natural outcome of groups of individuals with a common individual supremacy. If a group of people sharing a common political ideology comes together, for example, then the organization formed by this group of individuals will project the same sense of supremacy that each individual possesses, magnified to a horrific degree. Thus, wars come into being.

All wars are based on the belief that one group of people has supremacy over another. In religious wars, the antagonists believe that their conviction is the only true belief and that the evils of the other side must be eradicated. Each feels justified because each side "knows"

that their belief is true and the other is false. Thus Muslims, who follow the "real" truth, oppose Jews, whose "real" truth negates the Muslim's truth. And the Christian truth negates them both. The Buddhists believe they have a higher truth than the Christians do, but this belief is false according to the Hindus, who are proved wrong by the Sikhs, who in turn are proved wrong by the Muslims. Such ideological wrangling is absurd.

Wars based on economics or political ideology are substantially no different. If one country has more food, resources, or land than another, the inherent supremacy of the country with less is all that is necessary to justify war. If someone must starve, then it should be someone else. Political justifications for war are identical to religious justifications, except that the belief involves the righteousness of social rather than moral ideology.

Belief in our supremacy over all other beings justifies our possessiveness, greed, envy, and jealousy. And because we recognize that others mistakenly believe in their own supremacy, it is also the source of our fears. If we want to see the ego in its full flowering, in its glory, in its prime, we need only meditate on this ultimate sutra of Patanjali. It sheds a brilliant light on the core of our selves.

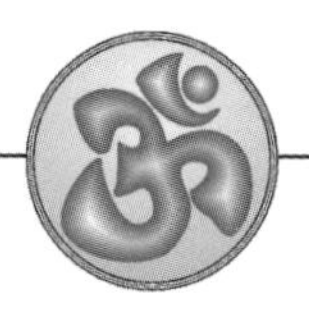

CHAPTER TEN

USING THE SUTRAS

I teach you the Superman. Man is something to be surpassed.

Friedrich Nietzsche
(1844–1900)

We have addressed only a few of Patanjali's sutras on attainment, but by now you may already grasp the spirit of his approach. If so, you can pursue the remainder on your own. For example, in reading the sutra on attaining the power to levitate, you might ask yourself if you are now in any way connected to the earth you would like to levitate above. If not, then clearly your task is to learn how to stop levitating, not how to begin. In reading the sutra on attaining the power to become tinier than an atom, you might want to inquire into just how large the substance of your self is at this moment.

Some of the sutras require historical knowledge in order to make sense of them. References to the sun, moon, or polestar, for example, refer to various centers within the body that were commonly known in Patanjali's time. If something makes no sense to you as you read the sutras, simply skip it and move on.

Numerous translations of the sutras are available, and choosing any one at random will more than likely serve you as well as any other, provided that the authors give their best account of a literal translation. If you want to be thorough, you may wish to acquire two or three versions and compare them. The sutras are short and generally an easy read.

After reading this little handbook, some may want to know whether, beyond what we have addressed, people really can learn to levitate, make themselves invisible, read minds, and the like. But surely the answer is unimportant. If you are able to make your body invisible, will it in any way help you to see your inner greed, envy, or fear? Will it bring awareness, compassion, and love into your life? Will it ease the suffering of your existence or bring any degree of peace into the world? These are the important issues, not the questions of invisibility or time travel. If you truly want answers to questions about the attainment of the physical powers, first find out who you truly are. The answer to any question you might still have about the powers will follow.

If, in spite of the above, you still have a burning desire to *know*, then you may look into the matter yourself. Appendix A describes the technique, called Samyama, that you must master to attain each of the powers; you apply this technique to various objects of perception in specific sequences. If you insist on pursuing

the objective reality of the powers, then read the technique, master it, apply it, and see for yourself. My advice, however, is identical to what Patanjali gives: Don't involve yourself in them, because you are wasting valuable time. If you attain the powers, you must relinquish them before you can proceed with living, because your ego is what has attained them, and attainment only makes the ego stronger. If you do not attain them, then you have poured energy into nothing. Nevertheless, you are free to do as you will. The choice is yours.

APPENDIX A

THE TECHNIQUE OF SAMYAMA

Patanjali goes into a fair amount of detail in describing how we can master this technique. It is a threefold process involving the following concepts:

1. Dharana
2. Dhyana
3. Samadhi

Their descriptions are as follows:

Dharana (Sutra 3.1)

Dharana can best be translated, in the context of Samyama, as "fixation." It involves a fixed attention of the mind on a single thought, concept, image, sound, or idea. It is a state where the mind is innocently held in a single place, a state where consciousness is naturally bound to one point or region. It is described by some as a steadfastness of concentration, though concentration in the context of Samyama is entirely without action of the will. Patanjali describes it as "directing the perceiving mind, with full attention, to a particular object or subject, either within the body or outside it."

Dharana is a natural state of the mind that you can observe on your own. Whenever we see danger, say a venomous snake in our path, our minds become fixed on the danger. No effort of will is required. The mind simply drops into dharana. The snake becomes the mind's total focus for a moment—it is concentrated, fully attentive to the reality of danger. Or if we catch a glimpse of a long lost loved one in a crowd, the mind drops naturally into dharana and we fixate on the movements of that person. All else momentarily disappears.

We can learn to enter the state of dharana by first observing ourselves when the state is naturally occurring. Silent observation of that state brings us to an understanding of it. It is through observation itself that understanding dawns, not through practice, effort, or technique. When we have understood the internal process that brings us to the state of dharana, then we have mastered it.

Dhyana (Sutra 3.2)

Dhyana can best be translated as "flow of thought." Patanjali describes dhyana as "An unbroken flow of thought toward the object of dharana, while in the state of dharana [as described in 3.1]." This is less complex than it sounds. If you have watched your thoughts with any degree of consistency you will have noticed that, for most of us, our thoughts never complete themselves. They are broken, confused, and unfocused. If you watch yourself while you are attempting to concentrate on any given subject, you will find that after only a few seconds your thoughts escape on a tangent. You will find yourself quickly considering a side issue or perhaps an entirely new subject altogether. Our thoughts are forever incomplete.

If we take the example of the venomous snake above, we may initially focus on the snake, but our thoughts quickly move to the issue of what to do with the snake. We are off to the future again; we have left the present moment. But if our thoughts remain with the snake itself, and the reality of the danger, then a change takes place. The problem is resolved without any thought of the solution. The full awareness of the problem itself is the means of solution. You must experience the magic of this for yourself in order reach an understanding.

Another example might be the problems of science or mathematics. As long as the scientist focuses on the problem itself, then his or her thoughts will remain unbroken. It is when thoughts of the solution enter that understanding of the problem ceases. If you watch yourself carefully as you approach any given problem you will see the state of dhyana occurring in its natural form. The occurrence may be brief, but if you are attentive you will catch it. It is a fullness of thinking—a continuity that is effortless and pure. You will also see its disappearance as you shift focus to the solution of the problem.

By observing the internal process that happens as we drift in and out of dhyana, we reach an understanding and dhyana becomes a part of our being.

Samadhi (Sutra 3.3)

Samadhi can best be translated as "absorption." Patanjali describes it thus: "Through dhyana and dharana one may reach the state where the object of focus engulfs consciousness, and the object appears as the subject. This is Samadhi."

Samadhi is a state where the line between the observer and the observed disappears. The thinker and the thought, the chooser and the choice, the actor and the act all become one movement. It is a state where reality is no longer distorted by the mind of the perceiver.

If we return to the example of the venomous snake, then when samadhi comes into being, a new perception dawns in which the relationship between the person and the snake changes. The snake is no longer a separate entity, and in this new relationship the concept of danger undergoes a radical transformation. In this state there is no longer a problem or a search for a solution, there is merely the reality of the snake.

Samadhi cannot be attained by will or discipline, both of which are aspects of the ego, because samadhi comes into being only when the ego ceases its existence. Samadhi is a natural outcome of dhyana. When the thought process, through its unbroken flow in dhyana, is allowed to complete itself it then comes to an end. That ending of thought is the ending of the ego.

Samyama

Sutra 3.4 describes Patanjali's concept of Samyama. He states that "When Dharana, Dhyana and Samadhi function together and are brought to bear on one subject, they are called Samyama."

Samyama is used in all of the Siddhis. By practicing Samyama on various objects of perception, sometimes in specific sequences, Patanjali tells us we can attain the specified powers.

For those interested in pursuing this further, Appendix B shows an example using Samyama in the context of the "Levitation" sutra.

APPENDIX B

SAMYAMA AND LEVITATION

Sutra 3.42 states:

"By practicing samyama on the relationship between the body and akasa, the body becomes as light as cotton fiber. The body can then levitate in space."

The word *akasa* describes an all-pervasive energized emptiness surrounding all solid objects. It is usually translated as "ether" or "space." An understanding of the implications of akasa is key to the understanding of this sutra.

If we practice dharana and dhyana on the concept of "space," what will happen? If you diligently apply yourself to this task, you will find that your experience of space is manufactured by thought. Space, like time, exists only in the realm of thinking.

We create space in the abstract when we conceive of individual objects separated by distance. Thus we imagine the space between planets, stars, and galaxies. But we cannot experience this space in any real manner whatsoever. It exists as formulas, geometric constructs, and images that we have internalized from books, school, and our own imaginings. Likewise we have created internal images of the space between New York and London, one person and another, or our home and the grocery store. You may have traveled from home to the grocery store, but if you are aware during the travel, you experience no sensation or awareness of space. Your belief that there is an intervening space is a creation of your thought process. You believe, for example, in the space within your room. But if the walls are removed, what meaning does that space have? What space exists that you can be aware of?

Space is created by thought as a way to separate your individuality from the rest of the world. If space can exist, then you can yourself exist as an isolated entity within this universe of space—you can have a separate existence. But this is an illusion. Through the practice of dharana and dhyana you can see this reality for yourself. You will also see that your experience of space is self-centered. You experience space as something extending outward from yourself. The distant mountain, the intervening trees, the friend at your side are all placed in space relative to your own body, which is always the center of space for yourself. Wherever you move, you are still the center of space. This is your experience.

Dharana and dhyana can show you the reality of your thought processes and your creation of images of the world. It can show you how you have yourself created space and time. But to go beyond the process of thinking and see the true nature of the relationship of your body to space, you must practice samyama. There is nothing that anyone can tell you about this true relationship because it has nothing to do with the realm of words and ideas. It must be discovered by yourself. And when it is discovered you will see that space is created through the process of separation, which is an illusion. Separation requires the existence of distinct objects that can be separated, and thus space between them is created. But through samyama you will find that there are no distinct objects, but merely a continuity of form. No one thing can be isolated from any other thing. Life and the material world are a single totality.

When the true nature of your body and its relationship with space are revealed, then you will have mastered levitation, and beyond that, movement through space in any direction or distance at will. The material effects of that are for you to discover.

List of Illustrations

Other Books by the Author

The Secret of the Yamas
A Spiritual Guide to Yoga

Into the Heart of Truth
The Spirit of Relational Yoga

The Fabric of Self
Meditations on Vanity and Love

Beyond the Siddhis